PRAYERS
For Pre-Schoolers

Written by
Beverly Capps Burgess

Illustrated by
Caleb Burgess

Library of Congress Number 92-132176
ISBN 1-879470-02-0
Published in the United States of America by
Burgess Publishing, Inc.
P.O. Box 520, Broken Arrow, Oklahoma 74013
A division of Bill and Beverly Capps Burgess Ministries, Inc.
Second Little Lamb Edition 1993

All Scripture quotations are taken from the King James Version of the Bible.
(Some of the Scripture verses are paraphrased.)

Publisher's Cataloging in Publication

Burgess, Beverly Capps.
Prayers for pre-schoolers / Beverly Capps Burgess ; illustrated by Caleb Burgess. -- 2nd ed.
p. cm.
Preassigned LCCN: 92-132176.
ISBN 1-879470-02-0

1. Children--Prayer-books and devotions--English. 2. [Prayer books and devotions.] I. Burgess, Caleb, ill. II. Title.

BV4870.B87 1993 242.682
QBI93-1215

PRAYERS
For Pre-Schoolers

When I am Sad...

Father,

Sometimes when things go wrong, it makes me hurt inside. I am glad that You are always with me. When I think of how much You love me, it makes me feel better. Your love makes the hurt go away. I know You care about how I feel. Thank You for making me happy again.

In Jesus' Name,
Amen

The joy of the Lord is my strength.
Nehemiah 8:10b

When I am Lonely...

Dear Father,

Thank You for being my friend. I know I am never alone because You are always with me. You will never leave me. Please send new friends to play with me; I will be kind to them and show them Your love.

In Jesus' Name,
Amen

I will never leave you or forsake you.
Hebrews 13:5b

When I am Sick...

Father,

Thank You for being so good to me and sending Your Son Jesus. Thank You that He took stripes upon His back that I could be healed. He took my sickness so I can be well and I thank You for my healing.

In Jesus' Name,
Amen

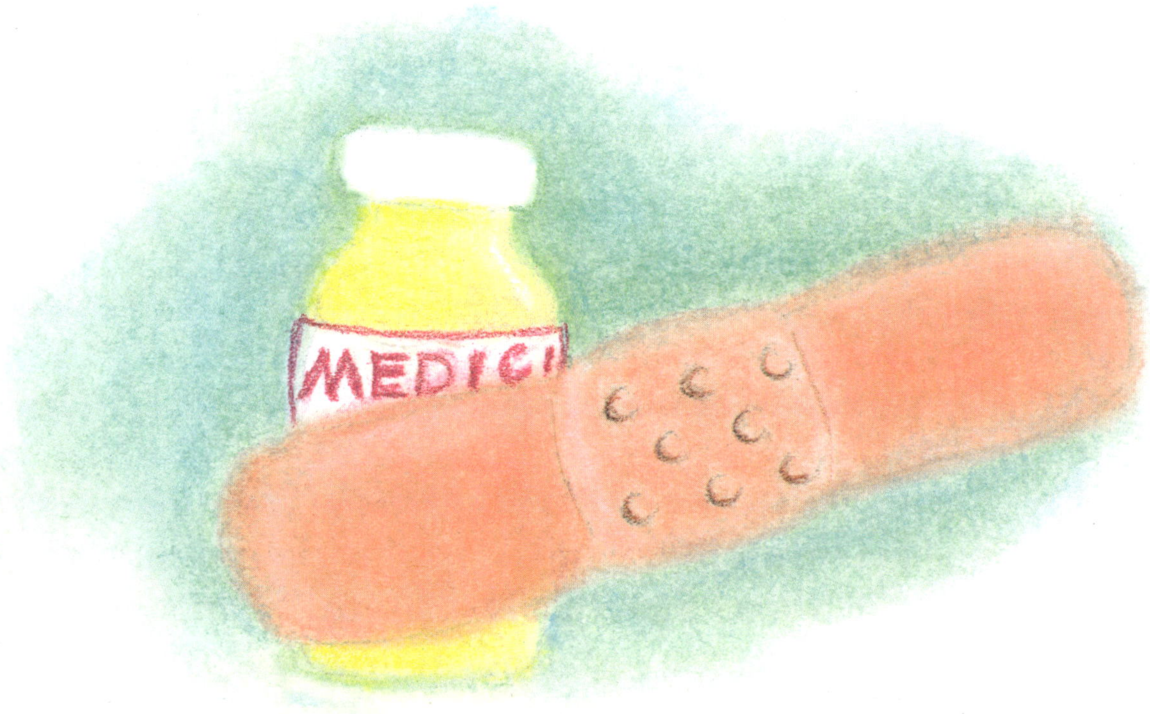

By His stripes I was healed.
I Peter 2:24

When I Need Forgiveness...

Father,

I am sorry because I did wrong. I want to obey You and my parents. Please forgive me. I love You so much. I will try my best not to make wrong choices. Please help me to remember Your Word. Thank You for forgiving me!

In Jesus' Name,
Amen

If we confess our sins, He is faithful and just to forgive us our sins...
I John 1:9a

When I am Afraid...

Father,

Thank You for watching over me. I know You see me all the time, even when I sleep. I don't have to be afraid because You will take care of me. You took care of Daniel in the lions' den and Jonah in the belly of the fish. I know You will protect me too. I do not have a spirit of fear, but of power, love, and a sound mind.

In Jesus' Name,
Amen

There shall no evil befall me...
Psalm 91:10a

When I Go to Sleep...

Father,

Thank You for giving us Your angels to watch over me and my family. Please help me rest well tonight and bless my family with sweet sleep. Help me to wake up full of joy tomorrow and to share Your love with others. I love You, God.

In Jesus Name,
Amen

For He shall give His angels charge over you, to keep you in all your ways.
Psalm 91:11

When I Wake Up...

Father,

Thank You for this day that You have made. I want to praise You with all that I say and do. Please help me to obey my parents and be a joy to them today. I really love You and I praise You with my whole heart.

In Jesus' Name
Amen

This is the day which the Lord hath made.
Psalm 118:24a

Before I Eat...

Dear Heavenly Father,

Thank You for always giving us good things to eat. Thank You for helping our bodies to grow strong and be healthy so we can serve You better. We praise You because You are so good.

In Jesus' Name,
Amen

But my God shall supply all your need according to His riches in glory by Christ Jesus.
Philippians 4:19

When I am Thankful...

Dear Father,

I am so thankful for all the good things You do for me. Thank You for my parents and my grandparents. Thank You for my home and my friends. I thank You for my church and most of all I thank You for loving me so much.

In Jesus' Name,
Amen

O give thanks unto the Lord, for He is good.
Psalm 107:1a

When I Want to Praise God...

Father,

You are so important. You created the whole world. You also made me! There is no one as wonderful as You. I love to sing praises and worship You. You are a very good God. I will honor You all my life. I really, really love You!

In Jesus' Name,
Amen

Praise ye the Lord...
Psalm 106:1a

When I Want To Ask Jesus Into My Heart...

Dear God,

I believe that You sent Your Son Jesus into the world to die for my sin. I want to make Jesus my Savior now. I am sorry for my sin and I know Jesus rose from the dead so I could be forgiven. I confess Jesus Christ as my Lord and I want to serve You forever.

In Jesus' Name,
Amen

That if thou shalt confess with thy mouth the Lord Jesus, and shalt believe in thine heart that God hath raised Him from the dead, thou shalt be saved.

Romans 10:9

When I Want To Pray for Others To Be Saved...

Dear Heavenly Father,

I pray for __________ that he/she would understand the Bible and that Jesus died on the cross for him/her. Please send someone to share Your Word with __________ soon. Thank You for Your goodness which will lead him/her to You.

In Jesus' Name,
Amen

Go ye into all the world and preach the gospel to every creature.
Mark 16:15b

When I am Worried...

Father,

I ask You to help me stop worrying about __________. I know that You love me and that I can't change things by worrying. Thank You for giving me peace. I trust You to take care of this problem.

In Jesus' Name,
Amen

Trust in the Lord with all thine heart...
Proverbs 3:5a

When I Want To Pray For My Church...

Father,

Thank You for giving me a good place to worship. I pray for our minister and I thank You that he hears Your voice and does Your will. Thank You that the people in our church love You and each other.

In Jesus' Name,
Amen

Love one another.
John 13:35